Chiang Mai Travel Guide 2024

Experience Chiang Mai, Thailand With The Ultimate Travel Preparation Manual To Thailand's Eternal City, Discover The Ancient History, Arts, Food and Culture Of Chiang Mai

Daryl Cass

Contents

INTRODUCTION

*T*ucked away in the northern Thai hug, Chiang Mai entices visitors with an allure that is timeless. A seamless blend of history and modernity emerges as the sun rises over the city's historic walls, creating an enchanting aura unique to this cultural sanctuary. Twenty-four years later, Chiang Mai is still evidence of its lasting influence. The sound of temple bells and the aroma of incense greet you as soon as you step foot in the city, setting the stage for an entrancing symphony of sensations.

Imagine meandering through the Old City's medieval alleyways, where centuries-old temples mutely tell stories of earlier times. The guardian mountain, Doi Suthep, stands sentry above the city and invites you to climb its slopes to take in expansive vistas that go on forever. Chiang Mai is a cultural patchwork created by the echoes of saffron-clad monks and the vivid colors of traditional fabrics.

Nevertheless, a contemporary pulse flows through the city in time with the old splendors. Chic cafés are all over the place, serving up a diverse array of dishes that include both traditional Thai fare and international cuisine. When the sun sets, the Night Bazaar comes to life, converting the streets into a vibrant tapestry of hues, scents, and the steady pace of everyday life.

This travel guide serves as your guide to all of Chiang Mai's many attractions. We shall celebrate the city's unique culture, untangle its complex past, and reveal the hidden gems that lie in store for daring adventurers via the pages that follow. Chiang Mai welcomes you with wide arms, regardless of your preference for the excitement of bustling marketplaces or the spiritual comfort found behind the walls of hollow temples. Accompany me on this literary trip into the heart of Chiang Mai, where each step reveals a new chapter in the history of this enduring city.

BRIEF HISTORY OF CHIANG MIA

*N*estled in Northern Thailand's hazy mountains, Chiang Mai is a city rich in history. Its elaborate temples, colorful alleyways, and age-old customs whisper stories of a magnificent history filled with victories and conflicts, as well as spiritual depth and cultural complexity. To fully comprehend Chiang Mai, one must go back in time and follow in the footsteps of the merchants, monks, and monarchs who established the city's distinctive character.

The Lanna Dawn: The ascension of King Mangrai in the thirteenth century marks the start of our tale. He established Chiang Mai, which translates to "New City," as the seat of the recently established Lanna Kingdom in 1296. Chiang Mai became the center of Lanna, the "Million Rice Fields," which covered what is now northern Thailand as well as portions of Myanmar and Laos. Due to its advantageous location on the Ping

River, a significant trading route, the city developed into a hub for both business and culture.

Lanna's Golden Age: Early Lannan rulers fostered a flourishing Theravada Buddhist culture. Beautiful temples with golden spires rising up to the sky were constructed, such as Wat Phra Singh and Wat Chedi Luang. At this peak of craftsmanship, master craftsmen produced exquisite lacquerware, silk fabrics, and wood sculptures that were well-known throughout Southeast Asia. Lanna literature and art flourished, showcasing the kingdom's rich religious life and affluence.

Difficult Times: But there were also negative aspects to Lanna's heyday. There was always danger from the Burmese Empire and the neighboring kingdoms of Ayutthaya (Siam). After Chiang Mai was overrun by the Burmese in 1558, an era of unrest and deterioration began. Burmese control suppressed Lanna's cultural expression and stunted the region's economic development for two centuries. The city's previous splendor vanished, and several temples sustained damage.

Rebirth and Metamorphosis: King Taksin of Siam freed Chiang Mai from Burma rule in 1774. Lanna progressively merged more and more into the Siamese monarchy, even as it maintained some autonomy. King Mongkut (Rama IV) brought about improvements in the 19th century that brought life to the city. Due to its advantageous position, Chiang Mai was vital to commerce with China and Burma, and its economy was further boosted in 1896 with the building of the Burma Road.

The 1900s and Later Years: Chiang Mai saw significant development in the 20th century. Trade and tourism were facilitated by the city's connection to the larger Siamese realm by the advent of the railway in 1922. New medical and educational methods were brought by Western missionaries, and their influence on the social structure of the city was long-lasting. After the Japanese occupation of Japan during the Second World War, there was a period of rapid modernization.

The Chiang Mai of today: Chiang Mai is a thriving city today, striking a balance between the energy of the present and its rich history. Travelers swarm to discover its historic temples, indulge in its cuisine, and hike across the magnificent mountains. The city's laid-back appeal and growing creative culture have drawn entrepreneurs and digital nomads from all over the world. But there are still difficulties. Key challenges confronting the city include striking a balance between development and conservation, protecting Lanna's cultural legacy while welcoming change, and guaranteeing fair growth for all of its residents.

A Tradition Carved in Stone: We are surrounded by ruins of Chiang Mai's illustrious past as we stroll through its streets. Every temple, every elaborately carved gateway, every busy market has a tale to tell. The friendly grins of the locals, their fervor for life, and their commitment to Buddhism are remnants of Lanna's spirit. Knowing the dates and details of Chiang Mai's past is not as important as appreciating the culture's tenacity, the elegance of its artwork and customs, and the people's lasting legacy. This little overview of Chiang Mai's past hardly begins to tell its fascinating tale. Every period has its own heroes and villains, secrets of its own. See the reflection of its golden period in the glittering eyes of its inhabitants, let its history speak to you, and listen to the whispers of the past in the rustling of the wind through ancient banyan trees if you really want to feel the charm of Chiang Mai.

CHAPTER 1

GETTING TO CHIANG MAI

PLANNING YOUR TRIP

*I*n 2024, first-time travelers will find Chiang Mai, the historic and cultural center of northern Thailand, to be an enticing destination. A vacation to Chiang Mai, which is well-known for its historic temples, bustling marketplaces, verdant scenery, and friendly locals, is sure to be enlightening and unforgettable. This book will cover a variety of topics to make sure your trip is exciting and full of cultural learning, from figuring out when to visit to checking out the local sites.

Choosing the Best Time to Visit: Since Chiang Mai has different seasons, it's important to plan your vacation at the right time. The most popular time of year is during the dry season, which runs from November to February. It provides a bright sky and pleasant temperatures. But it also implies that there will be more tourists. The shoulder seasons of March through June and September through October may be more appropriate if you're looking for less crowds. Remember that the Songkran Festival, which celebrates the Thai

New Year with a statewide water battle that brings mayhem and excitement to the streets, takes place in April.

Organizing Your Schedule

Making the most of your stay in Chiang Mai is certain when you create a well-rounded schedule. Start by seeing well-known temples like Wat Phra That Doi Suthep, Wat Chedi Luang, and Wat Phra Singh. Explore the Old City's winding lanes and alleyways to get a true sense of the native way of life. These are home to quaint shops, authentic teahouses, and galleries.

The highest mountain in Thailand, Doi Inthanon National Park, has amazing panoramic views, so think about incorporating a visit there. Interact with the local hill tribes to learn about their distinctive way of life, which will provide you with an educational and cultural experience.

Options for Accommodation

There is a wide variety of lodging available in Chiang Mai, ranging from luxurious resorts to inexpensive guesthouses. Consider staying in the Old City for convenient access to major sites or in the Nimmanhaemin neighborhood for a more modern and fashionable atmosphere, depending on your interests and budget. Authentic experiences may also be had in traditional Thai guesthouses, which are often encircled by peaceful gardens.

Chiang Mai Transportation

Chiang Mai is not too difficult to navigate. In the city, red songthaews, or shared taxis, and tuk-tuks are popular forms of transportation. Consider hiring a scooter if you want more freedom, but be aware of traffic and road conditions. There are also ride-sharing services like Grab accessible. Make your travel arrangements in advance, particularly if you want to visit places outside of the city.

Sensitivity to Culture

It's important to respect regional traditions and customs. Respect dress regulations by keeping your shoes on outside of temples and dressing modestly while entering places designated for worship. Remember that it is improper to show love in public and that holy places should be treated with the greatest respect.

Trying Out the Regional Cuisine

For foodies, Chiang Mai is a culinary paradise. Explore the thriving street food scene and indulge in regional specialties like mango sticky rice, northern Thai sausage, and curry noodle soup (soi). Take a gourmet trip around the Night Bazaar and experience a variety of flavors while taking in the vibrant environment.

Taking Part in Cultural Events

Incorporate cultural activities into your vacation to make it better. Learn the skill of making authentic Thai food by taking a traditional Thai cooking lesson, or enjoy a traditional Khantoke supper that includes northern Thai food and traditional dance performances. Participating in such activities with the locals helps one develop a stronger bond with Chiang Mai's diverse cultural fabric.

Outdoor Excursions

There are many outdoor activities available in Chiang Mai for those who love the outdoors. Set off on a hiking adventure across the verdant hills and forests around the city. Elephant sanctuaries provide a morally sound and informative experience that enables you to engage in responsible interactions with these magnificent animals.

Safety and Health

Put your health and safety first by keeping up with the latest developments in these areas. Maintain proper hydration, use sun protection, and exercise caution while handling food and liquids. Make sure your travel insurance includes coverage for medical situations, and get acquainted with the emergency services offered in the area.

Chiang Mai shopping

Make the most of Chiang Mai's distinctive shopping opportunities. Investigate the vibrant marketplaces, such the Sunday Night Walking Street Market and the Warorot Market. Find locally made textiles, artworks, and souvenirs to support local makers and bring a little of Chiang Mai's lively culture home.

Even though most people in tourist regions speak English, knowing a few simple Thai words can improve your visit and demonstrate your appreciation for the native way of life. The effort is valued by the locals, and it may result in more genuine encounters.

A first-time visitor to Chiang Mai in 2024 will need to carefully examine the ideal time to come, create a well-balanced itinerary, choose appropriate lodging, comprehend transit alternatives, and embrace cultural sensitivity. You will make lifelong memories in this charming city by being fully immersed in the local way of life, enjoying regional food, and participating in a variety of activities. You will leave Chiang Mai with a profound respect for Thailand's northern treasure thanks to its unique combination of culture and modernity. It promises to be a remarkable tour.

TRANSPORTATION WITHIN CHIANG MAI

*I*f your first encounter with traveling in Thailand was snarling through Bangkok traffic, Chiang Mai is going to surprise you in a good way. Explore this little city of stupas, temples, and marketplaces to find that Thailand's northern capital provides a more tranquil experience. Bound by a moat and the ruins of the city's medieval walls, Chiang Mai's ancient center is rationally laid out and has little traffic, making exploration simple. But heading out into the suburbs and beyond means figuring out a maze of congested highways and major streets. Many tourists get by just by renting a scooter or motorbike, but it's simpler to delegate the heavy lifting to a hired pickup truck.

The bustling assortment of marketplaces throughout the city is a prominent hindrance to effortless road navigation. Thanon Wualai is closed to traffic on Saturdays due to the Saturday walking street market, while Thanon Ratchadamnoen is closed on Sundays due to the Sunday walking street market. The Night Bazaar on Thanon Chang Khlan is another popular spot at night; most visitors are dropped off close by and explore on foot. These are the finest methods to travel about Chiang Mai, whether your plans are to stay in the city center or go out to the hot springs, waterfalls, botanical gardens, palaces, and wildlife sanctuaries in the nearby hills.

Traveling to and from the airport is affordable, simple, and quick.

As more people go to Thailand, Chiang Mai is becoming a more popular first point of call. Airport transfers are quick and affordable. A licenced airport taxi service to the old town departs from Chiang Mai International Airport at Exit 9 from the Arrivals hall; shuttle and minibus services are somewhat less expensive, while rideshare transfers via Uber or Grab are in the middle. Simply ask your hotel or guesthouse to set up a transport, call for a ridesharing, or signal a pickup truck as you're leaving Chiang Mai.

In Chiang Mai, the rót is the mainstay of urban mobility.

If you spend any time at all in Chiang Mai, you will eventually notice the throngs of red-clad pickup trucks that are constantly zipping around the streets. In the center, these vehicles, known as "red trucks" or rót , serve as shared taxis, picking up riders moving in the desired direction. Simply wave one down and inquire with the driver whether they are heading in your direction; routes aren't predetermined. A helpful idea is to hail a rót headed on one of the main routes that leave the city walls for visits beyond the historic center.

A rót is capable of more for you than that. For longer excursions out to the waterfalls, temples, elephant camps, and other sites in the hills covered in forest around Chiang Mai, drivers also charter out their cars. Although it will cost much more than a shared journey, a day excursion by rót may be surprisingly inexpensive when shared by many individuals. Chiang Mai's affordable downtown transportation alternative is the state-of-the-art bus system.

The RTC City Bus blue buses, which were introduced in 2018, provide a cheap and practical means of transportation across downtown Chiang Mai. These spacious, air-conditioned buses run nine routes, and the CM Transit smartphone app allows users to track services in real-time.

Each ride has a fixed cost of 20B, which may be paid with cash or the Rabbit stored-value card (get one at the airport's RTC kiosk and top it up at convenience shops). For lengthier excursions, go to the Arcade Bus Terminal close to the intersection of Thanon Kaew Nawarat and Route 11 for longer travels, or to the Chang Phueak Bus Terminal on Thanon Chotana (Thanon Chang Pheuak) for trips north of Chiang Mai Province. Additionally, shared pickups, or blue songthaew, are available to nearby towns.

Rickshaws and tuk-tuks are primarily for entertainment rather than for transportation (A to B).
The vibrant túk-túks (autorickshaws) of Chiang Mai provide charter transportation around the city. While they're more costly than rót , they're nevertheless quite popular with visitors, and drivers sometimes direct them to less healthy nightclubs and establishments that take

commission. Even so, it's a fun way to go through traffic in a partially open taxi with flashing coloured lights and the wind flowing through your hair. Strike a hard deal for a fair price. Samlors, or traditional cycle rickshaws, are still in use in certain areas of Chiang Mai, especially at the Talat Warorot market. Take a ride to preserve the custom; they are affordable and enjoyable.

Although they are cheap, taxis are not always simple to locate.

Although metered taxis are available in Chiang Mai, you won't often see them driving about the city. You may phone CnxTaxi Chiang Mai to hire a taxi while you're in town. Ridesharing services are simpler to locate since drivers are available in the area for both Uber and Grab, despite sporadic efforts to shut them down.

For simple day excursions outside of the city, rent a scooter.

Renting a motorbike or scooter allows you to explore a wide range of possible day outings, such the looping ride through the Mae Sa Valley and Samoeng, which is one of Thailand's most fun road rides, or visits to the well-known mountaintop temple at Wat Phra That Doi

Suthep. In addition, you may swim in rainforest waterfalls like Si Lanna National Park's "Sticky Waterfall" and explore the remains of the ancient capital of the Lanna kingdom at Wiang Kum Kam.

The southern portion of the old town is home to several rental agencies, the majority of which require you to leave your passport as security. Carry your driver's license, international driver's license, picture ID, and helmet at all times to prevent any issues with the law. Avoid taking a chance on motorcycles that some operators provide without insurance. You should, at minimum, have coverage for any injuries sustained in an accident involving you and other cars, as well as for any associated medical expenses.

Riding a bike is a terrific way to explore Doi Suthep's off-road trails and get about the city.
In Chiang Mai, renting bikes from stores and guesthouses is a simple task. They're perfect for strolling down the old town's more sedate routes, but be cautious if you enter the fast-moving, congested roadways that encircle the historic center. There, you'll be vying for

space with swift-moving buses, automobiles, motorbikes, and rót .

Try specialized mountain biking and cycle tour businesses like Chiang Mai Mountain Biking & Kayaks, Trailhead, and Spice Roads if you'd want to hire a better bike. The nearest downhill mountain bike routes are located in Doi Suthep-Pui National Park, which is situated just west of the city boundaries. Rental businesses may provide transportation for both you and your bike to the top of the trails, allowing you to concentrate on the exhilarating descent.

The easiest method to see the monasteries in the ancient city is on foot

Walking around the many wat (monasteries) in Chiang Mai's historic center is perhaps the best way to see them all, from well-known temples like Wat Chedi Luang, Wat Phan Tao, and Wat Phra Singh to more sedate monasteries hidden alongside lanes. When crossing the street, just be cautious of motorcyclists traveling at high speeds and rót . The marketplaces in Chiang Mai were likewise designed to be explored on two legs. On Saturdays and Sundays, Thanon Wualai and Thanon Ratchadamnoen are the "walking street" markets in

Chiang Mai, and it might seem as if everyone is strolling through them. Talat Warorot's bazaars are particularly interesting to explore on foot.

On the Mae Ping River, boat rides are solely recreational.

Apart from the well-liked tourist boats departing from Wat Chaimongkhon, south of the center on Thanon Charoen Prathet, not much passenger movement occurs these days, despite the fact that a lot of product still travels down the Mae Ping River to the market in Chiang Mai. Evening cruises are a popular option for a floating supper with a view, while daytime excursions wind through the city and proceed south to the ruins at Wiang Kum Kam.

In Chiang Mai, accessible modes of transportation

With the exception of the bustling pedestrian street markets, downtown Chiang Mai should be quite accessible on paper since it is mostly level and not very congested. Nevertheless, pavement ramps are not always functional, road crossings are not always accessible to the handicapped, pavements are often small and cluttered with obstructions (such as exposed drain covers), and many hotels—especially those on the lower end of the price range—have stairs instead of lifts. High-end establishments could be your only bet for really accessible accommodations. Wheelchairs can be accommodated on Chiang Mai's buses, but if you have a foldable wheelchair, renting a rót or minivan can be a more convenient option for you to travel about. Although locals would frequently go out of their way to assist guests in overcoming challenges, there are benefits to traveling with an able-bodied partner. Be aware that a lot of the monasteries in Chiang Mai have rough walkways and stairs for access, which might be difficult for those with mobility issues.

CHAPTER 2

ACCOMMODATION OPTIONS

Chiang Mai, the cultural center of northern Thailand, is renowned for its magnificent temples, antiquated customs, enthralling history, and spectacular natural scenery, which includes verdant rice fields, towering mountains, hypnotic waterfalls, and more. One of the most well-liked travel destinations in Thailand, this energetic city offers a wide range of sights and activities, as well as an equal number of choices for lodging. Don't worry, however; we'll provide you with all the information you need to choose the greatest places to stay in Chiang Mai, including the finest neighborhoods and hotels of all shapes and sizes. We are the professionals, after all; let us serve as your guide!

There isn't a simple or universal solution to the problem of what neighborhood is ideal for lodging during a trip to Chiang Mai. Instead, what's "best" depends on your own interests and tastes. The more information you have about each possible neighborhood, including its mood and points of interest, the better equipped you will be to choose the location and lodging that best fit your needs.

For instance, although history buffs may find the Old City's historic charms to be ideal, a more modern population may find greater appeal along Nimmanhaemin Road's hip cafés, galleries, and boutique stores. While those seeking a calm escape would like a place like Riverside, night owls will find great pleasure in the Night Bazaar's after-dark charms. Sanitham is the last destination; it's a refuge for tourists seeking a more authentic experience. Of course, it's also critical to choose a location and lodging that suits your budget. For each of the five Chiang Mai regions included in this guide, we've also included suggestions for the top low-cost, mid-range, and high-end lodging options.

1. THE OLD CITY

Chiang Mai's Old City, the historical capital of the Lanna Kingdom, has a rich history that is still visible in the ruins of the 700-year-old fortress walls around it that were formerly surrounded by a moat. You'll get the impression that you've traveled back in time as you stroll through the Old City's winding lanes, which are lined with historic sites, traditional wooden homes, and structures that date back hundreds of years.

Chiang Mai's Old City is a fascinating site that welcomes tourists to explore the old Thai customs, culture, spirituality, and architecture that have created the city, all thanks to its exceptional historical importance. The Old City is also home to a large number of contemporary stores, charming cafés, and art galleries. This contrast results in an enthralling blend of contemporary conveniences and vintage charm.

Because of its convenient position, the Old City offers quick access to a wide range of sights, lively marketplaces, captivating street scenes, and neighborhood restaurants that are all within walking distance. Meanwhile, this region has become known as a backpacker's center because to the abundance of reasonably priced lodging alternatives. For those who are visiting Chiang Mai for the first time, the Old City is a great destination. You may want to try someplace else if you're a frequent visitor or want to experience something more local.

BUDGET HOTELS IN OLD CITY

Thanks to its convenient Old City location,

Nai Wiang Poshtel: is peaceful, clean, and conveniently close to markets, temples, and other attractions. Free bikes are also included!

Rendezvous Classic House: is situated in an Old City neighbourhood that is both peaceful and practical. The large, opulent rooms and generous facilities of this traditional Lanna-style home belie its low cost. Rendezvous Classic House is a highly-liked choice because of its outdoor pool, substantial breakfasts, and welcoming staff; make sure to make reservations well in advance of your vacation.

The Hidden Garden Hostel: has free WiFi, an outdoor pool, and communal lounge in addition to a range of elegant but simple room types (all with air conditioning).

MID-RANGE OLD CITY HOTELS

The contemporary rooms of

Da Naga Hotel: are roomy and comfortable, and the hotel's traditional Thai architectural design mixes in harmoniously with its historic surroundings. well situated with the Tha Phae Gate just a short distance away. Two on-site restaurants, Nag Spa, a spa pool, Naga Art Gallery, an outdoor courtyard, and Thai cookery workshops are among the facilities and services offered.

U Chiang Mai: Situated on Ratchadamnoen Road,is a trendy and modern low-rise boutique hotel with a laid-back atmosphere and prime location. Take advantage of the elegant Resident's Lounge (located in the immaculately renovated old governor of Chiang Mai mansion), luxurious accommodations, friendly service, and the Sunday Walking Street Market just outside your door.

LUXURY HOTELS IN OLD CITY

99 A stunning hotel: with an unusual blend of the old and the contemporary is the Heritage Hotel. The hotel seems like a chic refuge despite being right in the heart of the Old City's bustle owing to its impeccable suites, gorgeous landscaping, exceptional service, and charming outside dining area surrounded by gardens and ponds.

Luxurious lodgings in Phra Singh Village, Chiang Mai's newest addition, are luxurious. Among the opulent lodging options in Old City, Phra Singh Village stands out for its large rooms, verdant surroundings, cozy wood and terracotta furnishings, kind service, and superb food.

The Inside House: is the height of luxury lodging. Tucked away in a lush tropical setting in the center of Chiang Mai, this tranquil retreat has all the ambiance and decor of a 1920s Lanna Colonial manse. Select from beautifully designed bedrooms and suites with pools.
View All Chiang Mai Hotels

2. ROAD NIMMANHAEMIN

This upscale neighborhood, which also happens to be the business hub of the city, is well-liked by couples and business travelers looking for sophisticated urban experiences. It has a vibrant and modern vibe. This is made possible by trendy cafés, fashionable shops, and hip art galleries that feature a wide variety of modern and traditional Thai artwork. Nimmanhaemin Road is a haven for epicurean explorers as well as art and culture aficionados. There is definitely something to suit every taste, from quaint breakfast cafes to global fusion restaurants to laid-back late-night eating that is well-liked by students from the neighboring Chiang Mai University.

 The neighborhood comes alive after dark with a thriving nightlife scene that includes live music venues, energetic nightclubs, neighborhood drinking places, and evocative rooftop pubs. If you choose to stay in the Nimmanhaemin Road neighborhood, you will have prime access to this popular destination. Nimmanhaemin Road may not be the ideal choice if you'd rather be somewhere a little further off the main path. Comfortable housing alternatives are available to accommodate a variety of needs and tastes, and they are all conveniently located near local attractions.

BUDGET HOTELS ON NIMMANHAEMIN ROAD

BED Nimman: The only huge outdoor pool in the neighborhood, attentive service, free bottled water, fruit, and cup noodles are all features of the adults-only.

Ibis Styles Chiang Mai: The 208-room is a "design economy" hotel that strikes a balance between affordability and quality with its hip location, international cuisine, free WiFi, and welcome drinks.

HOTEL NIMMANHAEMIN ROAD MID-RANGE

De Chai the Oriental: is a tranquil haven with sweeping views of Doi Suthep. This lovely hotel in the Colonial style has an excellent position only a short stroll from Old Town.

Zivi Nimman is a tiny boutique hotel with unique accommodations, complimentary breakfast, and lovely indoor-outdoor common areas—all in an exceptional location.

LUXURIOUS HOTELS ON NIMMANHAEMIN ROAD

Akyra Manor Chiang Mai: Intimate boutique hotel with cool downtown vibes, infinity pool and rooftop bar, views of the mountains and design-focused suites.

The unique U Nimman Chiang Mai: is a 147-room hideaway with opulent accommodations, a state-of-the-art fitness center, a wine bar with library and a tranquil garden area.

3. THE RIVERSIDE

The Riverside neighborhood of Chiang Mai, which is located on the banks of the Ping River, offers a peaceful haven from the busy city centre. Not that Riverside is drowsy, mind you. It is, instead, a neighborhood that combines the greatest aspects of both worlds—natural beauty with an international, cosmopolitan ambiance. You may anticipate taking leisurely strolls along the serene riverside promenade while visiting Riverside.
In search of something a little more thrilling?

Visit one of the numerous markets in the area to take advantage of the opportunity to sample delicious street cuisine and peruse handcrafted goods manufactured nearby while taking in the genuine ambiance.

Excellent restaurants serving anything from Thai delicacies to foreign food can be found at Riverside, many of which have beautiful views of the surrounding lake. In Riverside, there are luxury riverside resorts, boutique hotels, and hostels. For those looking for peace and quiet, the neighborhood is a great option because of its easy going appeal. A different neighborhood could be better if you're looking for a holiday with non stop excitement and nightlife.

CHEAP HOTELS IN RIVERSIDE

A delightfully rustic Thai-style hotel, **Rustic River Boutique** is conveniently located near the Old City, Night Bazaar, and other attractions. It has friendly personnel and a generous amount of facilities.

A distinctive teak wood guesthouse, ***Baan Songjum*** offers reasonably priced accommodations, a kind host, and a satisfying continental breakfast.

MID-RANGE HOTELS IN RIVERSIDE

The tranquil ***RarinJinda Wellness Spa Resort*** has a swimming pool, a spa, and lovely views of the river. It is a wellness-focused hotel. Sleek and contemporary, ***Hotel Ping Silhouette is*** a business-friendly hotel with free afternoon tea service, international food served in an on-site restaurant with garden views, and spa facilities.

LUXURY HOTELS IN RIVERSIDE

Nestled in the center of Lanna, **the Anantara Chiang Mai Resort** offers an opulent retreat. Its strikingly contemporary design combines traditional Thai and colonial components with floor-to-ceiling doors, balcony daybeds, Thai boxing, culinary lessons, and spa treatments to provide something for everyone looking for fun and relaxation. With a manager's reception complimentary every day, deep soaking tubs, an on-site spa, and other deluxe facilities, ***137 Pillars House*** has all you could ask for in a luxurious hotel. Admirers of the red carpet treatment will enjoy the lavish facilities and top-notch service at this magnificent five-star boutique hotel.

4. SANTITHAM

This charming, developing neighborhood is situated northwest of the Old City and has a variety of residential neighborhoods and local markets. A vibrant mix of locals, foreigners, and digital nomads, this lesser-known neighborhood provides a window into real, daily life in Chiang Mai. Santitham is particularly well-known for its international eating scene, which offers a range of cuisines including Thai street food, western foods, and fusion fare, as well as immersive cultural experiences like Thai cookery and language workshops.

The housing options in Santitham vary from affordable mid-range hotels to simple guesthouses, satisfying a variety of preferences and price ranges. Santitham is reasonably priced and intriguing while being conveniently located near Old City and other well-known Chiang Mai attractions. The neighborhood is also less frequented by visitors. There's no better place to find a relaxed local atmosphere than Santitham. Perhaps a different neighborhood would be better suitable for those who are attracted to touristic or faster-paced places (you won't find much English signs here).

BUDGET HOTELS IN SANTITHAM

Run by a kind family, ***Kitti Rose Home*** is a charming guest home that is pleased to assist with suggestions and bookings. ***Smile House Boutique's*** peaceful but handy location and lovely pool make it a great option for travelers on a tight budget. Budget boutique hotel ***B2 Santitham*** has warm, inviting rooms. An extra benefit? The great restaurant just across the road.

MID-RANGE HOTELS

in ***Santitham POR*** *The modest, boutique hotel* Santitham offers free water, coffee, and tea, as well as a lovely pool area, tidy, minimalistic rooms, and friendly *service.*

The Mercure Chiang Mai has a good gym, a beautiful rooftop pool, and rooms that are roomy and pleasant.

The Itsy Hotel has everything you might desire in a chic, minimalist hotel, including excellent service, a welcoming pool, and a co-working area that's perfect for digital nomads.

5. THE NIGHT MARKET

To the east of the Old City, spanning many city blocks, Chiang Mai's Night Bazaar is mostly known for its after-hours activities. During the day, this bustling neighborhood consists of a variety of shops, eateries, and lodging establishments, but at night, it transforms into one of Thailand's most well-known markets. This one-mile strip offers exciting encounters with a sprawl of merchants and street food stalls offering anything from exquisite silks and smart phone accessories to fruit smoothies and grilled meats. Even while the main street may draw your attention, as you go around the market, be sure to look down the tiny alleys; you never know what kind of hidden gems you could find there.

A wide variety of budget, midrange, and luxury hotels can be found at the Night Bazaar, making it the perfect destination for thrill-seeking urbanites (and bargain seekers!). We don't only intend to state that the Night Bazaar neighborhood has everything; a Starbucks is included. After your excursion to the Night Bazaar, you could prefer going home to a different neighborhood if you're searching for a more local or relaxed feel. My spouse and I stayed two blocks away from this location while we were there. Every night, we came, ate gyozas and purchased some clothes—we even were warned that our $2 pair of elephant trousers was overpriced. Make sure you get some! You could buy them with different kinds of protein, and they cost one dollar for six of them. Except for McDonald's, which was the same price as it is back home, food is much less expensive than I would have expected; reportedly, this is a delicacy.

NIGHT BAZAAR LOW-COST HOTELS

A reasonably priced hotel, Hotel **RCN Court & Inn** is located close to the Night Bazaar, Wat Buppharam Temple, and other attractions. Adorable and tidy, **Sridonchai Heritage Night Bazaar** Chiang Mai is well situated among the neighborhood's eateries and bars.

MID-RANGE NIGHT BAZAAR HOTELS

The Duangtawan Hotel is a well-liked choice because of its wonderful pool and bar area, large, spotless rooms and ideal position in the center of the Night Bazaar.

The DusitD2 is a contemporary hotel with large rooms (many with floor to ceiling windows and views of the city and mountains), exquisite décor, and unmatched Thai friendliness. The well-appointed rooms, spa, and rooftop pool of the Lana-style boutique hotel *Raming Lodge Hotel & Spa are its main features.*

LUXURIOUS HOTELS AT NIGHT BAZAAR

An urban resort ideal for families is Shangri-La. With a focus on minimalist luxury, its 277 rooms and suites have stylish Northern Thai décor, with plenty of teakwood, silks, and original artwork. A huge pool (complete with a slide!), spa, fitness club, and much more are available to you. The five-star Le Meridien Chiang Mai is a lavish establishment that combines contemporary Thai design and hospitality with European heritage. Luxurious accommodations with views of the city and mountains, a variety of dining choices, top-notch spa services, and a cool outdoor plunge pool are all available. *The gorgeous Maladee Rendezvous Hotel in Chiang Mai* is a quaint historic property with a gorgeous pool and pool area, soaking tubs, and a serene atmosphere. An ideal concealed haven situated in an unparalleled setting.

CHAPTER 3

LANDMARKS AND ATTRACTIONS

Chiang Mai has it all: breathtaking mist-covered mountains, intriguing hill tribes, and an amazing haven for travelers seeking something new. Despite its little size, it offers a wealth of activities, sights, flavors, and experiences. It served as the old Lanna Kingdom's capital when it was founded in 1296. These days, you can discover both the past and the present there, together with historic temples nestled among contemporary structures. Here are some of the best things to do in Chiang Mai that you should definitely schedule some time to explore.

1. SINGH WAT PHRA

The oldest Buddhist temple in the nation is this one. This historical site in Chiang Mai goes back to 1385. You must include it on your list of things to visit because of the amazing décor, gold-toned antique patterns, and a chapel with the footprints of Buddha. The golden Pagoda is also quite magnificent.

2. TREK FROM BAAN PJA DANG TO HUAY KUKAP

The greatest hiking trips are those that go from Baan Pha Dang to Huay Kukap. The three-hour hikes start with the well-known meditation cliffs and go through the unique highlands. It's an amazing drive with many views along the route, including a slowly running stream and little settlements. Seeing the peasants' way of life up close is, in fact, the highlight of the walk. Because of the knowledgeable guides, treks are appropriate even for those who have never gone.

3. THE GIBBON'S FLIGHT

This well-known zip-lining business is now active in Chiang Mai. Take a zip-line tour across the rainforests from above. This location offers excellent safety ratings, a committed staff, and the ideal means of getting some adrenaline throughout your visit.

4. ELEPHANT CONSERVATION CENTRE OF THAILAND

Do you want more elephants? For them, Chiang Mai is the ideal destination! Since its founding in 1993, this conservation organization has drawn a lot of attention. This area is home to about fifty elephants. It's amazing to see the elephants here perform on musical instruments and paint.

5. NIGHT BAZAAR AT KAT RIN KHAM

If you want to escape the other visitors, this less well-known night market is great. Though there are lots of delicious food vendors to keep you full, you can also purchase clothing, home goods, handicrafts, and more here. Although the merchants are typically open to haggling, the prices are quite low here. This Chiang Mai destination is the place to go if you want a fantastic flavor of Thai culture and some excellent souvenirs to take home. It has a younger, hipper feel since it's located across from the university.

6. THE NATIONAL PARK OF DOI INTHANON

This is a must-see sight in Chiang Mai if you like adventure. It links to the Doi Inthanon mountains in this park, which are a part of the Himalayas. These sights are breathtaking. This place offers a breathtaking dawn experience that will make you feel grateful to be alive, if you can wake early enough. As you stroll along the pathways, the waterfalls enhance the enchantment. See the stupas of Phra Mahathat Naphamethanidon and Naphamethanidon; also worth visiting are Brichinda Cave and the rare bird species.

7. NIGHT BAZAAR IN CHIANG MAI

The market to visit is the Chiang Mai Night market. Everyone visits there because of the amazing shopping and restaurants there. Although the others are worth seeing, this one is not to be missed. It has a certain appeal that sets it apart from other things. You can haggle for the finest deals on everything you can think of, from gadgets to accessories and everything in between, at this enjoyable location to shop. Additionally, some of the city's greatest street cuisine is located right here.

8. THE KALARE NIGHT MARKET

Outside of the local community, this is more of an underground market that is unknown to most people. It's a less busy area with gift shops interspersed with jewelry stores and art studios. Yes, there is also plenty of food. However, the Thai dance acts are one of the main attractions. Getting a personalized drawing of yourself made by local artists is a terrific purchase here.

9. TIGER MOUND

Do you want to see further animals? You can take in the Indochinese tiger conservation efforts at this Chiang Mai site. Since birth, they have all been reared in captivity so that you may have the opportunity to come to know these amazing animals. You may choose to make this location a stop on your schedule or camp here for the night if that's more your style.

10. THE ELEPHANT NATURE PARK

Elephant Nature Park is a special initiative that was started in the 1990s and functions as an elephant sanctuary and rescue facility. It has successfully rescued several distressed elephants from all throughout Thailand since its founding. In addition, it acts as a refuge for various animals, including dogs, cats, buffaloes, and more. This attraction in Chiang Mai ought to be at the top of your list if you're searching for a morally responsible location to see elephants. Time magazine honored the creator, Sangdeaun Lek Chailert, sometimes referred to as Lek, the Asian Hero of the Year for 2005.

11. ELEPHANT SAVE AND RESCUE CENTER IN RANTONG

The goal of this elephant conservatory is to assist in the rescue of mistreated elephants. They provide them a new, better life as well as a lovely, caring place to dwell. You may participate in a programme that lasts one day or many days to engage with the elephants. Taking care of an infant elephant is one of the highlights of your stay here. Additionally, white water rafting is an option here if you're seeking even more exhilaration.

12. SUTHEP DOI

By far the most well-known site in Chiang Mai is Doi Suthep. In addition to offering breathtaking vistas, this mountain is home to a 13th-century temple known as Wat Phra That Doi Suthep. It contains an Emerald

Buddha copy in addition to a large white elephant temple.

13. ROAD NIMMANHAEMIN

But Chiang Mai has more to offer than just elephants and temples. In Chiang Mai, this avenue is the hip area. Together with a multiplex theater and a luxury shopping center, you'll discover classy pubs and restaurants. This is the place to go if you want to see a movie in Thai or if you're temporarily in the area and are missing home in the West.

14. RIVER MAE PING

A boat trip down the Mae Ping River is a great way to spend a day in Chiang Mai. The teak buildings and verdant surroundings seem to drift past. Some trips include lunch at a local farmer's home, where you may have a really laid-back experience and get a flavor of rural Thai life.

15. AMBIENCE

Animal enthusiasts will like Chiang Mai. In between tigers and elephants, and now the Cat Café. It has a cat and UFO motif and is dubbed Catmosphere. The major attraction, however, is getting to view and stroke the kitties as you savor standard café fare.

16. CHIANG MAI GRAND CANYON

This Chiang Mai attraction isn't particularly well-known yet, despite its magnitude. It used to be a dirt quarry that flooded, but nowadays it offers some amazing vistas. Now that it has rained, the water is rather deep. Other than taking in the vistas, there isn't much to do here, but the visit is definitely worthwhile.

17. THE WAT CHEDI LUANG

The Temple of the Big Stupa is another name for this site in Chiang Mai. Here are the remnants of a once spectacular old temple. It was the original Emerald Buddha's residence. The temple was damaged after an earthquake in 1545, but it took the Burmese more than five years to demolish it. It is nonetheless a bustling place of worship in spite of this.

18. BAI BUTTERFLY AND ORCHID FARM

Thailand is represented by the orchid. See orchids in bloom and purchase gold-dipped flowers as mementos at this serene location. It's a beautiful site to visit in Chiang Mai, with a butterfly farm just next door.

19. PADUNG VILLAGE'S KAREN LONG NECK TRIBE

Originally from Myanmar, the Karen ethnic tribe escaped to Thailand, where they now reside in tiny settlements. A great method to see a simpler way of life is to visit the villages. If you want to interact with the locals, find out more about their everyday life, and buy their handicrafts, it's better to do this with a tour guide.

20. LOI KRATHONG FESTIVAL (BRIDGE OF of NAWARAT)

You're in luck if the Loi Krathong Festival is taking place in Chiang Mai. The 12th lunar month is used to mark this occasion. During the occasion, candles are placed inside baskets, known as "krathongs," which are fashioned like lotuses. In homage to Buddha, they let them float away in the moat. It's a clever and endearing event to be a part of, since the sky is also filled with lanterns launched into the air for good luck and known as the Yi Peng Festival (that is conducted simultaneously).

21. NIGHT SAFARI IN CHIANG'S MAI

This is an absolutely fantastic sight in Chiang Mai. At the Savanna Night Safari, visitors may ride an open tram and witness water buffalo, white rhinos, and kangaroos. Once again from a tram, you may witness wolves, lions, tigers, and crocodiles at the Predator Prowl Zone. It's an interesting location, and later in the evening, there's a light and music display that's well worth the wait.

22. HOT SPRINGS OF SAN KAMPHAENG

These hot springs in a forested location near the mountains are said to have therapeutic properties because of their high sulfur concentration. You can have a complete Thai massage, which is an unusual and soothing experience, and you can get eggs to boil in water for a good, nutritious meal.

23. THE SONGKRAN CELEBRATION AT THA PAE GATE

This Thailand New Year celebration, which takes place in April from the 13th to the 15th, is another event not to be missed if you chance to be in town; however, in Chiang Mai, it usually lasts longer. Prepare to be drenched since the idea is that tossing water will wash away your sins. It's also cool in the summertime.

24. WHAT IS RATCHAMONTHIAN?

There are many names for this temple, so don't be confused. Across from Wat Lok Molee is a hidden treasure called Wat Ratchamonthian, also known as Wat Rajamontean. Compared to other temples in Chiang Mai, this one is smaller and more serene, and it is immediately recognised by the enormous Buddha statue located in the courtyard. There is a smaller, lavishly gold-ornate Buddha in the main hall, which is constructed of wood. This is a really calm spot to meditate, and it makes it much more significant to be able to do it in the company of praying monks.

25. COMPLETELY NEW FIELD PRODUCT

A well-known café called Brand New Field Good is surrounded by paddy fields. Originally constructed as a wedding venue by a well-known TV personality, the space was subsequently transformed into a themed café and restaurant. This space, surrounded by greenery, has a serene, restful atmosphere that is enhanced by the use of natural materials for the lighting and décor. You should definitely try their excellent coffee and nice genuine Thai food while you're here.

It's a Thailand location that offers everything for everyone, with welcoming people, a plethora of marketplaces, opportunities to see elephants, mouthwatering cuisine, and even exhilarating activities thrown in for good measure. The best way to experience the culture is to try to visit Chiang Mai during the festivals, however there will be more visitors and hotels will fill up quickly. It should be easy to have a great time at one of Chiang Mai's numerous attractions, no matter when you come!

CHAPTER 4

CULINARY DELIGHTS

Searching for mouthwatering food in Chiang Mai that won't break the bank? You're going to like this! This little city is a budget-friendly foodie's dream come true as well as a refuge for cultural vultures.

Delicious alternatives that won't break the bank may be found in Chiang Mai, from fragrant street carts to modest restaurants nestled away in little lanes. Let's explore the greatest affordable dishes this city has to offer and indulge in the gastronomic wonders that lie ahead.

PAD THAI

40–60 THB is the average cost per serving.

Pad thai (row 664), a well-liked staple, is a Thai noodle dish that masterfully combines sweet and savory tastes. With the addition of eggs, tofu or prawns, bean sprouts and a variety of spices, stir-fried rice noodles produce a delectable symphony of flavors with every mouthful.

This dish, which is garnished with crushed peanuts and a squeeze of lime, is a must-try for any visitor to Chiang

Mai on a tight budget since it's not only a delicious meal but also reasonably priced.

Local Tip: Look for establishments that let you add extras like extra veggies or prawns to your pad thai. In this manner, you may have a customized and genuine rendition of this well-loved meal.

KHAO SOI

Cost per serving on average: 80–150 THB

Khao soi will take your taste buds on a culinary tour through the essence of Northern Thai food. This aromatic and filling curry noodle soup is a well-balanced combination of soft and crispy noodles, thick, coconut-based broth, and tender meat, usually chicken or beef. This dish, which has Burmese culinary origins, is served with shallots, cilantro, lime, pickled mustard, ginger, and chili paste as accompaniments.

This dish is offered in local cafes and reflects the culinary (row 748) tradition of Chiang Mai with its distinctive blend of textures and tastes.

Go explore the old town or local marketplaces, such as Warorot Market, to discover soi from family-run stands.

Local Tip tip: You can get this specific street cuisine in Chiang Mai at a number of restaurants all across the city. That being said, we heartily suggest having it at the well-known, Michelin-starred Khao Soi Maesai restaurant.

Do not be afraid to request more chili paste if you want it hotter!

GREEN PAPAYA SALAD, OR SOM TUM,

typically costs between 30 and 50 THB per dish. Som tum is the solution for those who are in the mood for a spicy and cool pleasure. Shredded green papaya, cherry tomatoes, green beans, peanuts, and chilies are combined in this colorful Thai salad along with a zesty and hot vinaigrette.

Local TIP: Look for vendors that produce something fresh upon request. The burst of flavors and the delightful crunch of fresh veggies make som tum a popular and refreshing street food alternative. To customize the meal to your liking, choose the sweetness and degree of spice.

And think about having som tum as an accompaniment to heartier Thai dishes.

ROTI

Average price per dish for: 50–100 THB

Roti is a humble yet delicious delicacy that originated in the streets of Chiang Mai and has won over many hearts. Exquisitely crafted, thin layers of dough are deep-fried till golden, and then presented with an assortment of garnishes, including chocolate, bananas, condensed milk and even savory alternatives like gammon and egg.

For those venturing into the local culinary scene, roti is a great treat because of its cost and adaptability.

Local tip: Try roti, which are made in front of you by experienced sellers at night markets or on street corners. Try combining various tops and fillings, such as egg and gammon or banana and condensed milk.

MOO PING (GRILLED PORK SKEWERS):

20 to 30 THB per dish on average

You need go no farther than moo ping for a pleasant and savory snack when the mood strikes. These soft, marinated pork skewers have a delicious smokey taste and a touch of sweetness from the marinade. They are cooked to absolute perfection.

Moo ping is a fast and affordable way to have delicious grilled beef on the move while exploring the streets of Chiang Mai. It is sometimes served with a side of sticky rice.

Local Advice: Look for moo ping at night time street food vendors or local markets. Make sure the skewers are cooked through by keeping an eye on them as they grill. Remember to dip them in the sauce that is supplied for an additional taste boost!

THE COCONUT PANCAKES, KHANOM KROK

20–40 THB is the average cost per serving.

Khanom   is a wonderful and adorable street food that will satisfy your sweet taste. These little candies are proof positive that wonderful things can come in little packages. These little, bite-sized coconut pancakes are made with a crispy outside and a creamy inside thanks to the use of a specifically crafted skillet. Khanom Krok, drenched with a hint of coconut cream, is a cheap and delectable delicacy to enjoy while exploring Chiang Mai's streets. It has the ideal ratio of tastes and textures.

Local Tip; Since it is often manufactured in large quantities early in the day, check out the morning markets for fresher options. The quality   is distinguished by its crispy edges and creamy interior.

FRIED RICE, OR KHAO PAD

Cost per serving on average: 30 to 50 THB

The flavors of pad are like a carnival in your tongue; each bite offers a unique combination of flavors and textures that will make your taste senses dance joyfully. It's a mixture of rice, eggs, veggies, and your preferred protein—usually tofu, prawns, or chicken—all together! This meal is also perfectly stir-fried with flavorful sauces and spices. In our minds, a pad is more than simply a dish—it's a blank canvas onto which each chef paints their own unique masterpiece. You may discover variations that satisfy your tastes wherever you go, from the busy marketplaces to the peaceful nooks of neighborhood

CHICKEN FRIED IN GAI TOD

20–40 THB is the average cost per serving.

Thai-style crispy fried chicken, or tod, has a crispy exterior and a tender inside. It's a well-liked street food choice with an enticing blend of flavors and textures that is marinated in a mixture of spices and then perfectly fried. Not to mention the dipping sauces! Your taste senses will be treated to a flavorful dance as a result of those zesty, spicy partners that take the experience to whole new heights.

Local advice: Grab some tod from street sellers or local markets for a quick snack. To get that extra crispy texture, look for suppliers that maintain a high oil temperature.

SAI OUA (NORTHERN THAI SAUSAGE)

20 to 40 THB on average per dish

Sai is a fragrant, tasty banger packed with regional herbs and spices that will introduce you to the distinct flavors of Northern Thai cuisine. With the addition of red curry paste, kaffir lime leaves and lemongrass, this coarsely ground pork sausage takes on a unique flavor that is somewhat spicy and savory.

Sai provides a flavor of genuineness and is often served with sticky rice and fresh veggies. If you want to make your own, be sure to dry the sausage enough after filling it to get that perfect crispy texture. Slicing the sausage into pieces and frying them will give them a delicious crunch during cooking. Finally, use fresh galangal and lemongrass, since these will improve the taste profile considerably.

Local advice: For a genuine taste of sai , visit Chiang Mai's wet markets or traditional food vendors.

KANOM JEEN NAM NGIAW (RICE NOODLES WITH CURRY)

40–70 THB is the average cost per serving.

A meal you just must try is   nam , for a heartier gastronomic experience. This Northern Thai speciality is served with soft rice noodles in a flavorful, creamy curry broth made with tomatoes. You'll receive a blast of tastes that represent the different elements of the area, much like its name, which is fairly mouthful. A variety of toppings, such minced pork, fresh herbs, and pig ribs, are placed on top.

And even with its nuanced flavor, kanom nam ngiaw is still popular among those who are keen to sample Chiang Mai's distinctive cuisine.

Local advice: For an authentic taste of kanom jeen nam , check out the morning markets or local restaurants. Savor the richness of the curry sauce and the high caliber of the ingredients as you dine.

BRAISED PORK LEG OVER RICE, OR KHAO KHA MOO

averages 40 to 60 THB per serve.

One meal that exemplifies the skill of slow-cooked perfection is khao kha moo. A bed of steamed rice is served with a luscious and soft pig leg that has been cooked to a fall-apart tenderness. A hard-boiled egg, pickled mustard greens, and a side of rich gravy are often served with the meal.

Local advice: Savour khao kha moo in quaint, family-run restaurants that specialize in slow-cooked cuisine. To improve the meal, if you're feeling really daring, consider requesting extra toppings like crispy pig skin or a soft-boiled egg.

JOK (RICE PORRIDGE)

costs 20 to 40 THB on average per serve.

Jok is helpful when looking for simplicity and comfort. This comforting bowl of deliciousness, rice porridge, is produced by slowly boiling rice until it takes on a creamy, velvety consistency. Jok is often eaten for breakfast or as a light supper. It may be modified by adding different toppings, such as chopped ginger, green onions, minced pork, and soy sauce.

Native Advice: Try jok as a breakfast choice to feel like a native. Seek for suppliers that prepare their rice porridge to a creamy smoothness.

TOM YUM GOONG, OR SPICY PRAWN SOUP

typically costs between 50 and 80 THB per bowl.

With tom yum goong, a well-known Thai soup that balances sour, spicy, and savory flavors, be ready for a flavor explosion. This fragrant soup is made with tender prawns, mushrooms, galangal, lemongrass and kaffir lime leaves cooked in a tart broth. Because of its strong tastes, it's a popular option for those looking for a spicy boost without going over budget.

Local Tip: Try the tom yum goong at respectable eateries that place a strong focus on using fresh ingredients. Observe how the tastes of sour, spicy, and savory are balanced.

RICE SOUP, KHAO TOM

20–40 THB is the average cost per serving.
Thai comfort cuisine is best summed up as one simple, but very filling dish: khao tom. It's a transparent, light rice soup that's often eaten for breakfast or as a comfort food. Khao tom is a filling dish that has modest components like rice, veggies, and your choice of protein (such chicken, pig, or fish). Its subtle taste combination is pleasing.

Local Advice: Accept khao tom as a hearty morning meal. Look for neighborhood restaurants that provide this tasty yet straightforward rice soup.

KAI KROK (EGGS FROM QUAIL)

20–30 THB is the average cost per serving.
A popular street meal in Chiang Mai, kai krok has a delicious texture contrast, with a crunchy outside and a creamy yolk within. It's perfectly prepared on a

well-seasoned classic cast iron khanom krok pan. The heat from the griddle guarantees that the egg whites are cooked through and the yolks become semi-soft but still delicate.

Drizzled over the eggs to enhance their flavour profile are a substantial portion of pepper powder and a special Thai spice sauce. An extra spicy bite may be added with a splash of Sriracha sauce for those with a daring palette. Kai is a speciality that can be found at busy markets and food stands. It makes a tasty and convenient snack.

Local advice: Visit nearby marketplaces like Warorot or Somphet Market for a true taste of kai krok. Seek for vendors that have a constant flow of patrons to guarantee the freshest and most delicious experience.

CHAPTER 5

SHOPPING IN CHIANG MAI

*T*here's no better way to get a taste of a place than via its food. Fortunately, Chiang Mai has a wide variety of night markets where you may purchase a wide range of locally made goods, including apparel, accessories, souvenirs, and tasty and affordable cuisine. I've visited a number of night markets in Thailand, but without a question, the greatest are in Chiang Mai! Here is a list of the top 8 night markets in Chiang Mai, Thailand, in case you plan to visit the region in the near future.

CHIANG MAI'S SUNDAY NIGHT MARKET (THA PHAE WALKING STREET)

Open Sundays from 5 to 10.30 p.m.

The Sunday Night Market, also known as Tha Phae Walking Street, is by far the largest and most well-liked night market in Chiang Mai and is a must-see. From Tha Phae Gate to Wat Phra Singh Temple, the whole stretch of Rachadamnoen Road is home to the market. Because there is so much to see, you will definitely be wandering up and down the market many times, so I strongly advise wearing comfortable shoes. Hundreds of kiosks offering inexpensive clothing and locally made goods, ranging from fridge magnets to more unusual mementos, may be found here. Even an area where you can receive a massage for only 100 baht is available! The food courts of Chiang Mai's Sunday Night Market are located within temple grounds, which is what makes it so fascinating. There are seats and tables set up, but arrive early since it may be difficult to secure a space later. Note that you're not permitted to consume alcohol or smoke during the Sunday Night Market. The Sunday Night Market is only open on Sundays from 5 p.m. to 10.30 p.m., as its name implies.

CHIANG MAI'S SATURDAY NIGHT MARKET (WUALAI WALKING STREET)

Opening hours on Saturdays are 5–10 p.m.

Wua Lai Walking Street, also known as the Saturday Night Market, is Chiang Mai's second most well-liked night market. The night market starts at Chiang Mai Gate Market (see below) and continues for a significant stretch down Wua Lai Road. Although it's a little smaller than the Sunday Night Market, the items for sale are comparable. Additionally, there's a place where you can get a massage, and while I was there, I even spotted a few street performers. I also suggest going to the Silver Temple while you're there, since it is remarkably open on Saturdays until 11 p.m. The temple, which is bathed in blue lights, is a sight to see at night and a must-see attraction when in the city.As with the Sunday Night Market, it is not permitted to smoke or consume alcohol. Only on Saturdays from 5 p.m. to 10 p.m. is the Saturday Night Market open.

MARKET NEAR THE SOUTH GATE OF CHIANG MAI GATE

Opening times: everyday from 4 p.m. to 2 a.m.
I suggest going to the Chiang Mai Gate Market, which is held at the south gate on both sides of Bumrung Buri Road, if you aren't lucky enough to visit Chiang Mai on a weekend. If you're seeking a midnight snack, this is the ideal spot to go. It's open every day from 4 p.m. till late. The Chiang Mai Gate Market mostly offers food, but if you go on a Saturday, you may also find some shops selling apparel and trinkets. There's one Khao Soi vendor here that's very excellent and affordable,

beginning at 50 baht just. It is impossible to overlook since it is close to the crossing. I also paid 25 baht for two fresh mangoes, 50 baht for a large pancake and 10 baht for a bunch of sweets. As you can see, if you're searching for some tasty and affordable cuisine in Chiang Mai, this is unquestionably the finest spot to go.

CHIANG MAI NIGHT BAZAAR

is open every day from 5 p.m. to 12 a.m.

Changklan Road is restricted to traffic every day from 5 p.m. to midnight in order to host the Chiang Mai Night Bazaar, where local sellers offer a wide range of items, including clothing, accessories, souvenirs, and handicrafts made in the area.I suggest going between 6-7 p.m. when most vendors are open and it's not too busy.The bustle of Chiang Mai Night Bazaar is outdoors, where rows of vendors cover both sides of Changklan Road. There is an inside market with a few shops offering food and trinkets. Unlike the weekend markets in Chiang Mai, this place allows alcohol, and there are several pubs that offer happy hour specials.

KALARE EVENING MARKET

Opening times: everyday from 5 to 11.30 p.m.

Go to Klare Night Market if you're seeking somewhere to dine while enjoying Chiang Mai Night Bazaar. Essentially, it's a food court with around 20 vendors and a dining space in the center. A few merchants selling clothing, trinkets, and artwork may also be found in the rear and close to the entrance.On the positive side, there's more room to sit and eat, and sometimes there's live music. I thought the food here was a little more costly than at the weekend night markets. In addition, there's an area where massages are available for 100 baht.

ANUSARN NIGHT MARKET

Open everyday from 5 p.m. until 11 p.m.

This enormous covered market, which is open every day and has a large assortment of apparel, accessories, and souvenir vendors, is also close to the Chiang Mai Night Bazaar.There is plenty of room to move about, and to keep things from seeming too hot and crowded, ceiling fans are installed.Chill Square is a food court located in the center of the market where you can get inexpensive beer and Thai cuisine. At the very end of the night market, there are a few pubs and food vendors as well.

PAVILION NIGHT MARKET

Open everyday from 5 p.m. until 11 p.m.

With just a few dozen shops, Pavilion Night Bazaar is among the smaller night markets in Chiang Mai that we have included. There aren't many tables and chairs since it's tiny, so if you want to snag an empty table, get there early. Even though not much is happening here, if you're already in Chiang Mai Night Bazaar or Anusarn Night Market, it's worth a brief stop.

CHIANG MAI UNIVERSITY NIGHT MARKET

Open everyday from 5 p.m. until 11 p.m.

The Chiang Mai University Night Market is ideal for those seeking a more authentic local experience since it's less frequented by tourists and is situated outside of the Old Town, approximately a 20-minute drive away. It has a food court area, many apparel boutiques, and a covered area with vendors selling more goods and trinkets. With shirts priced as little as 80 baht and dresses as much as 250 baht, the clothing is reasonably priced and of good quality.

Advice for Those Visiting the Night Markets in Chiang Mai

About one to two hours after their official opening times, the Chiang Mai night markets are livelier and more entertaining to visit. You may visit all three night markets in one evening since they are located on the same road as the Chiang Mai Night Bazaar: the Klare Night Market, the Anusarn Night Market, and the Pavilion Night Bazaar. Most of the night markets are only accessible by foot. At the entrance and exit are songthaews (red buses) and tuk tuks if you require transportation back to your accommodation. As an alternative, you might use Grab cab service or

CHAPTER 6

FESTIVAL AND EVENTS

ANNUAL CELEBRATION

Chiang Mai, which is tucked away among Thailand's gorgeous mountains, is a vibrant, living city. Even with all of the beautiful temples, vibrant marketplaces, and delicious food, the city's spirit is best shown during its yearly festivals. These celebrations are more than just tourist attractions; they are an intricate part of Lanna culture, with each colorful thread narrating a tale of dedication, ancestry, and camaraderie.

1. Loy Krathong and Yi Peng, November:
During Yi Peng, hundreds of sky lanterns, or "khom loi," shoot up like heavenly fires as the full moon casts a silvery radiance across the sky. This show, which takes place the day before Loy Krathong, represents welcoming good fortune and letting go of negativity. Rivers and lakes glisten with many handcrafted krathongs on Loy Krathong itself, which are little floating boats bearing gifts and wishes. Seeing these bright lights create a breathtaking display in the night sky.

2. April's Songkran:

Songkran is a wild water battle that celebrates the Thai New Year. The streets become colorful water battlegrounds where both residents and visitors splash one other with exuberant enthusiasm. The splashing of water in a lighthearted manner represents a new beginning and the removal of ill luck. Be prepared to be drenched, embrace the spirit of fun, and feel the warmth of Thai hospitality at its finest.

3. San Kamphaeng Handicrafts & Bo Sang Umbrella Festival (January):

This colorful festival celebrates the creativity of Bo Sang hamlet, which is well-known for its gorgeous paper umbrellas, and is held on the third weekend of January. Take in colorful handcraft exhibits, see detailed demonstrations of producing umbrellas, and immerse yourself in the bright ambiance. Don't pass up the opportunity to get a one-of-a-kind memento that is lovingly made by hand and embodies Lanna heritage.

4. February's Chiang Mai Flower Festival:

With the arrival of warmer weather, Chiang Mai bursts into a riot of color during the Flower Festival. The streets of the city are transformed into a breathtaking flower garden. Take in the magnificent parades, take part in floral design workshops, and breathe in the heady scent of an endless supply of flowers. This event is a beautiful celebration of the beauty of nature and a feast for the senses.

5. May is Visakha Bucha Day:

Visakha Bucha Day is very important to pious Buddhists. It honors the Buddha's conception, realization, and demise, all of which took place on the sixth lunar month's full moon day. With lighted processions, chanting monks, and a calm, devotional atmosphere, temples come to life. On this fortunate day, engage in merit-making activities, give alms to monks, and enjoy the tranquil calm that permeates the city.

Outside the Festivities:

There are several smaller festivities held across Chiang Mai throughout the year, but these main festivals are what bring tourists from all over the world. There's always plenty to do and see, from the yearly World Elephant Day celebration at the Elephant Nature Park to the nearby temple festivals and merit-making rituals.

Take part in the One-Kin Street Food Festival to fully experience the native cuisine, or visit Wat Phra Singh to see the vibrant Lanna Loy Kratong.

A Guide to Enjoying Chiang Mai's Festivities:

* **Plan your trip:** Research the dates of festivals you'd like to attend and book your accommodation well in advance, especially during peak season.

 * **Respect local customs:** Dress modestly if visiting temples, avoid boisterous behavior during religious ceremonies, and be mindful of local cultural norms. * **Embrace the spirit of fun:** Let loose, participate in the festivities, and don't be afraid to get involved. The people are kind and like sharing their customs with guests.

* **Support local artisans:** Buying trinkets from handicraft markets and stalls can help to maintain Lanna customs and the local economy in addition to allowing you to bring a piece of Chiang Mai home.

The yearly festivals in Chiang Mai are not just must-see events for visitors, but also vivid windows into the heart of the city. Every celebration has a distinct vibrancy that highlights the diverse fabric of Lanna culture, religious fervor, and camaraderie. Bring an open mind, an inquisitive heart, and a readiness to fully experience Chiang Mai's beauty when you arrive. The genuine spirit of Chiang Mai is found not only in its sights and sounds but also in its lively pulse, as you will find when you watch the sky lit up with lanterns, take part in the joyful water wars, and perform time-honored customs.

SPECIAL EVENT CALENDAR

Nestled amid Thailand's breathtaking mountains, the dynamic city of Chiang Mai is alive with activity. Beautiful temples, bustling markets, and mouthwatering cuisine notwithstanding, the city's soul is most fully shown during its annual festivities. These festivals are more than just tourist traps; they represent an intricate aspect of Lanna culture, with each vibrant thread telling a story of commitment, heritage, and friendship.

1. November, Loy Krathong and Yi Peng:

During Yi Peng, the full moon shines a silvery brightness over the sky, causing hundreds of sky lanterns, or "khom loi," to spring up like heavenly flames. The day before Loy Krathong, this spectacle symbolizes embracing good fortune and letting go of negativity. Many handmade krathongs on Loy Krathong itself, which are little floating boats containing presents and wishes, sparkle in the rivers and lakes. Observing these brilliant lights provide an amazing show in the night sky.

2. Songkran in April:

A chaotic water fight known as Songkran is held to commemorate the Thai New Year. The streets turn into vibrant water battlegrounds as locals and tourists wildly splash at one other. Lighthearted water splashing is symbolic of a fresh start and the banishing of bad luck. Get ready to get wet, enjoy the good times, and experience the best of Thai hospitality.

3. Bo Sang Umbrella Festival & San Kamphaeng Handicrafts:

This vibrant event, which takes place on the third weekend of January, honors the inventiveness of the Bo Sang hamlet, which is well-known for its exquisite paper umbrellas. Admire vibrant handicraft displays, see in-depth explanations of how to make umbrellas, and take in the airy atmosphere. Don't miss the chance to get a unique keepsake that is painstakingly crafted by hand and represents Lanna hi

4. Chiang Mai Flower Festival, February:

During the Flower Festival, Chiang Mai explodes in color as warmer weather arrives. The city's streets are turned into an exquisite flower paradise. Take in the gorgeous parades, take part in floral creation workshops, and breathe in the rich aroma of an infinite supply of flowers. This occasion is a visual feast for the senses and a lovely celebration of the splendor of nature.

5. Visakha Bucha Day is in May:

For devout Buddhists, Visakha Bucha Day is highly significant. It commemorates the full moon day of the sixth lunar month, which was the day of the Buddha's conception, realization, and death. Temples come to life with lighting processions, chanting monks, and a serene, spiritual ambiance. Give alms to monks, participate in merit-making activities, and take in the peaceful atmosphere that pervades the city on this auspicious day.

Away from the Celebrations:

While Chiang Mai has a number of lesser celebrations all year long, it's these major events that draw visitors from across the globe. From the annual World Elephant Day celebration at the Elephant Nature Park to the neighboring temple festivals and merit-making ceremonies, there's always something to see and do. To truly enjoy the local food, attend the One-Kin Street

Food Festival, or go to Wat Phra Singh to witness the colorful Lanna Loy Kratong.

A Handbook for Savouring Chiang Mai's Celebrations:

Arrange your travel: Look up the dates of the festivals you want to go to and reserve your lodging well in advance, especially during the busiest times of the year.

Respect local customs: When visiting temples, dress modestly, refrain from acting rowdily during religious ceremonies, and be aware of local cultural norms. **Embrace the spirit of fun:** Have fun, join in the festivities, and don't be afraid to get involved. The locals are kind and like showing visitors their traditions.

***Adopt local craftspeople:** Purchasing souvenirs from artisan markets and stalls not only lets you take a piece of Chiang Mai home, but it also supports the local economy and Lanna culture.

Not only are Chiang Mai's annual festivals events that tourists should not miss, but they also provide vibrant windows into the city's core. Every festival has a unique energy that showcases the unity, religious fervor, and diversity of Lanna culture. When you visit, bring an open mind, an inquiring heart, and the willingness to truly appreciate Chiang Mai's natural beauty. The true essence of Chiang Mai can be felt in its vibrant pulse as well as its sights and sounds, as you will discover when you see the sky filled with lanterns, participate in happy water fights, and carry out age-old traditions.

CHAPTER 7

DAY TRIPS AND EXCURSIONS

NEARBY ATTRACTIONS

*T*hailand's "Rose of the North," Chiang Mai, entices with its historic temples, colorful marketplaces, and verdant mountain scenery. Discover the abundance of natural beauties and cultural pearls in the surrounding area, in addition to the city itself, which offers a treasure trove of experiences. So, lace up your shoes, pack your appetite for adventure, and let's dig into some enthralling day trips and excursions from Chiang Mai, all conquerable in under 24 hours.

Doi Inthanon National Park: Embracing Nature
Doi Inthanon National Park, the crown gem of Chiang Mai, is home to Doi Inthanon, Thailand's highest mountain. Climb to the top for breath-taking views, or meander amid colorful flower beds and tumbling waterfalls. Hike through lush forests, take in the glistening splendor of the Twin Pagodas, or visit Hmong hill tribal settlements to immerse yourself in their distinctive customs. Don't miss Wachirathan Waterfall, a tribute to the majesty of nature with its tumbling

beauty. Keep in mind that the temperature drops at the peak, so bring layers.

Temple Trails: Beyond Doi Suthep

Climb the narrow path to the summit of Doi Suthep mountain, where you will find Chiang Mai's most venerated temple, Wat Phra That Doi Suthep. Glistening golden pagodas stand among elaborate paintings and expansive cityscapes. Take a walk in the nearby woodland or take a cable car ride down for a thrilling blast of excitement. Discover Wat Umong, tucked down behind a system of subterranean tunnels, or Wat Chiang Man, the oldest temple in the city, for a little peace and quiet. Take in the mystical atmosphere of these hallowed places.

Hill Tribes and the Golden Triangle: Cultural Tapestry

Travel north to the confluence of Laos, Myanmar, and Thailand, known as the Golden Triangle. See the majestic Mekong River, explore neighborhood marketplaces full with hand-crafted finds, and discover the intriguing background of the opium trade. Discover more about the several hill tribes that call this area home to get a greater understanding of local life. Discover the distinctive customs and traditions of each tribe by visiting Karen longhouses, seeing Lisu fire dances, and meeting Akha people dressed in vibrant beads.

Ethical Sanctuaries: Elephant Encounters

Visit elephant sanctuaries where the goal is to rescue and rehabilitate these gentle giants and experience a slower pace of life. Take part in ethical feeding and washing sessions, see their fun character, and educate yourself about their condition. Steer clear of riding elephants, put their welfare first, and choose sanctuaries that are dedicated to their protection. Recall that ethical travel guarantees contented elephants.

Creative Wonders: Chiang Rai and White Temple

Spend a day excursion to Chiang Rai to see the eerie splendor of Wat Rong Khun, often known as the "White Temple." This modern marvel defies conventional temple architecture with its shimmering mosaic tiles and unusual sculptures. Take in the bizarre displays of the Black House Museum, stroll around Chiang Rai's

106

lively Saturday Night Market, or pay a visit to Wat Doi Mae Nak, a shrine honoring a sad love tale.

Adventure Playground: Waterfalls and Zip Lines

Sex-seekers, get comfortable! Experience exhilarating zip lines over the rainforest canopy, feeling your heart race as you take in the stunning aerial vistas. Follow waterfalls like Huay Mae Klang Lang and Mae Sa for a cool excursion. These undiscovered gems are ideal for swimming and having picnics in the shade of the dense vegetation. If you want to experience another culture, visit the ancient Lanna villages tucked away among the rice terraces.

Delicious Haven: Lanna Cooking and More

Without sampling some of Chiang Mai's delectable cuisine, a visit is not complete. Try the flavorful and creamy Khao Soi soup or Khantoke, a traditional Lanna feast served on short tables piled high with vibrant foods. Discover the vibrant Night Bazaar, which is a refuge for street food sellers serving regional specialties. Don't miss Chiang Mai's famed sticky rice and mango dessert, a delightful end to your gourmet trip.

Out of the Ordinary: Cooking Classes and Night Safari

Experience a nighttime experience at the Chiang Mai Night Safari, where you can see nocturnal animals coming to life under the starry sky. Take in a moonlit display of intriguing animals, elephants taking a bath, and tigers prowling. Take a traditional Lanna cooking lesson for a hands-on learning opportunity. Discover how to make flavorful stir-fries, curries, and desserts, then bring these culinary techniques home as a delectable memento.

These day tours and outings provide just a small sample of the colorful tapestry that envelops Chiang Mai. Travelers seeking the embrace of nature, spiritual enlightenment, cultural immersion, or thrilling experiences may find something to suit their needs in the surrounding area of Chiang Mai. So prepare to uncover the hidden treasures that are lying just beyond the city walls by packing your luggage, grabbing your spirit of adventure, and getting going.

Keep in mind:

* Select excursions and activities from moral providers who emphasize ecotourism and sustainable travel.

* When visiting temples and villages, abide by the customs and traditions of the area.

* When you attend places of worship, dress modestly.

OUTDOOR ADVENTURES

---

*T*he "Rose of the North," Chiang Mai, is more than simply a city of vibrant marketplaces and historic temples. Located in the northern region of Thailand, between beautiful valleys and lush mountains, this destination is a refuge for outdoor lovers, offering an alluring combination of thrilling activities and tranquil natural beauty. There is enough to interest every traveler in Chiang Mai, regardless of experience level.

Exploring Verdant Jungles:

* **National Park of Doi Inthanon:** Doi Inthanon, Thailand's tallest peak, is a hiker's dream come true. Explore tumbling waterfalls, trek through hazy jungles, and take in breath-taking views from the peak.

* **National Park of Doi Suthep Pui:** Explore this park that encircles Doi Suthep mountain while hiking among historic ruins and seeing entertaining macaques. The journey to the exquisitely mosaic-adorned Wat Pha

Lat temple rewards you with breathtaking views of the city.

* *The Caves at Chiang Dao*: Venture out on a cavern exploration in the Chiang Dao area. Discover historical Buddhist artifacts and explore undiscovered caverns decorated with stalactites and stalagmites.

Exhilaration on Two Wheels:

* **Trail Cycling:** Follow difficult mountain paths via rice terraces and deep woods. Enjoy stunning vistas while traveling on mild inclines or exhilarating descents.

* **Crater Biking Experiences:** Take a guided bike excursion to discover paths that are less traveled. Explore bamboo woods, come across small communities, and take in the peace and quiet of the countryside.

Delicious Waters:

Rafting on Whitewater: Navigate the exhilarating swirls and bends of the Mae Taeng River while canoeing through breathtaking landscapes. This heart-pounding trip is ideal for parties looking for a once-in-a-lifetime encounter.

*** Canoeing and Kayaking:** Cruise the Mae Ping River while taking in the peace and quiet of the surrounding scenery and a variety of wildlife. Discover undiscovered bays and mangrove forests while taking in a tranquil getaway from the metropolis.

****Separate Occasions:****

* ****National Elephant Preserve:**** Learn about responsible elephant tourism by visiting an ethical elephant sanctuary. Take in the sights of these gentle giants in their natural environment, helping to ensure their survival and welfare.

* * *Spiraling through the Forest:*** Take on a thrilling zipline experience as you soar over the trees. Experience the wind in your hair as you zoom through canyons and get a unique look at the forest canopy.

Extracurricular Activities:

The outdoor experiences in Chiang Mai are just getting started. Enjoy a great local meal at a crowded night market, relax with a traditional Thai massage, or take in the colorful cultural scene after a day of touring.

Organizing Your Trip to Chiang Mai:

* **Optimal time to visit:** November through February is the chilly season, which is best for outdoor activities. That being said, Chiang Mai is lovely all year round, having a distinct charm for each season.

* **Getting about:** One common way to get around the city and its environs is by renting a motorcycle. There are also plenty of taxis and tuk-tuks available.

* **Room assignment:** There are several alternatives available, ranging from opulent resorts tucked away in the highlands to guesthouses that are affordable.

Keep in mind:

When visiting temples or rural regions, please respect local customs and dress modestly. Choose tour companies that uphold environmental protection and animal welfare responsibly. Because the environment may be unpredictable, particularly during the rainy season, it is advisable to pack for all eventualities.

With its plethora of outdoor activities, breathtaking scenery, and rich cultural legacy, Chiang Mai guarantees every visitor an amazing journey. Put on your hiking boots, take out your paddle, and get ready to enjoy the breathtaking scenery and exciting experiences of northern Thailand!

CHAPTER 8

PRACTICAL INFORMATION

USEFUL PHRASES

---

*T*he "Rose of the North," Chiang Mai, entices with its historic temples, verdant forests, and lively street markets. Knowing a few essential words in Lanna, the regional dialect, may, nevertheless, unlock doors like magic if you want to really enjoy the experience.

** Salutations and Etiquette:**

* **Khob Khun:** Thank you (Formal: Khob Khun Khrap/Ka) * **Sawasdee:** Hello (Formal: Sawasdee Khrap - male, Sawasdee Ka - female)
* **Chai:** Yes (Informal: Mai Chai - No) * **Chan Mai Dai Ma?:** I (Chan - informal, Phom - formal) How are you? (Formal: * **Chok Dee:** Good luck, Khun Sabai Dee Mai Khrap/Ka?) (Former: Khrap/Ka Chok Dee Khop Khrap)

Market Excursions:
* **Nee Tao Rai?:** How much is this? (Tao Rai Khrap/Ka?) in formal terms

118

* **Lorb:** Rebate * **Yim Neung Naa:** I'll take this (Formal: Yim Neung Nee Krap/Ka) * **Khon Gad/Mai Khon Gad:** Spicy/Not spicy * **Aroi Mak Mak:** Very tasty

Transportation:

Pai Nee?: What's the location? (Formal: Where is... located? - Pai Nee Tee-Nai...)

Roo Pai..: I'm heading... In formal terms, Chan Pai Tee-Nai

* **Ngee Nai Yang?:** Could you bring me to...? (Formal: Pai Tee-Nai Khun Yahng Chan...? Would you kindly take me to...)

* **Jor Thee Nai?:** How much is the tuk-tuk? (Original: Jor Thee Thai Rai Khrap/Ka?) Nai Nee

* **Yor Dee:** Move on now Formal: Yee Nee Khrap/Ka Yor Dee Tee

Religious Courtesies:

* **Krap/Ka:** Please/Thank you (used for offerings) * **Wat:** Temple * **Wihaan:** Shrine room * **Phra Buddha:** Buddha image * **Wai:** Customary

greeting with hands together and slight bow (display respect)

* Moderator Yaa Dee Dee: I hope you are blessed with good fortune and luck.

Delicious Foods:

Khan: Settle in ** **Aroi:** Tasty ** **Pet Mak:** Extremely spicy **Wan Noi/Wan Ngek:** A tad bit more/a tad less **Yam:** Spicy and sour salad **Khao Soi:** Well-known Chiang Mai noodle dish **Sai Oua:** Grilled sausage **Khan Tok:** Customary communal dining at a low table

Further Advice:

* **Grin!** Friendly smiles are a common characteristic of Thai people. * Speak clearly and gently. * Don't raise your voice.
* To show respect, conclude most sentences with "Khrap" for males and "Ka" for women.
* * Avoid touching people's heads. Wear modest clothing when you visit temples.

Acquiring these fundamental expressions will enrich your conversations with locals and lead to a wealth of cross-cultural understanding. Keep in mind that expressing respect and admiration for the Lanna tradition may be done with only a few words. Now inhale deeply, say "Sawasdee," and plunge straight into Chiang Mai's colorful tapestry!

Extra Words:

* **Kor Toat Nai?:** Could you please assist me? *
Chan Yoo Tee Rai: I don't understand.
* **Chan Rak Chiang Mai:** Chiang Mai is a city I adore!

Your trip to Chiang Mai will be very memorable if you take this guide with you and have a grin on your face!

CURRENCY AND BANKING

---

*T*ravelers are drawn to Chiang Mai, Thailand's charming Rose of the North, by its historic temples, lively marketplaces, and easygoing atmosphere. To have a worry-free and seamless experience, it is essential that you acquaint yourself with the local currency and banking system prior to succumbing to its allure. With the information in this book, you'll be able to handle baht and banks in Chiang Mai and concentrate on enjoying your trip.

The Mighty Baht: Chiang Mai's Gateway to You
In Chiang Mai, the Thai baht (THB) is the currency of choice, so exchange your money first. While big currencies like USD and EUR are frequently accepted at tourist sites, having some baht ready can open doors to smaller stores, street sellers, and local experiences.

Translating Your Money:
* **Exchange Bureaus for Currencies:** The city is full with exchange bureaus, particularly in the area around

Old Town and Thapae Gate. Prior to making a decision, compare prices and steer clear of locations that charge more. Mr. Pierre Money Exchange and Super Rich Exchange are two well-liked choices.

* **Bank ATMs:** ATMs are widely distributed around the city and provide easy access to cash withdrawals. But be mindful of the costs associated with withdrawals from the Thai bank as well as your own. For reduced costs, think about using ATMs connected to your bank.

* **Banks:** Although banks provide foreign exchange services, their rates may not be as favorable as those of bureaus. They do well, therefore, in more complicated currency trades and bigger transactions.

Best Advice: Keep a few smaller notes (20, 50, and 100 baht) on hand for routine purchases like street food and tuk-tuk trips.

Chiang Mai banking:
* **Creating a Bank Account:** If you plan to be in the area for a long time, you should think about creating a local bank account. This makes receiving transfers,

paying bills, and taking out cash easier. These may vary, but usually include your proof of residency, passport, and visa.

* **Debit and Credit Cards:** Major credit cards like Visa and Mastercard are generally accepted in Chiang Mai. To prevent transactions from being banned, let your bank know about your trip schedule. ATMs accept debit cards, but be aware of the costs.

* **International Money Transfers:** Convenient money transfers from overseas are available via services like Western Union and Wise. Prior to selecting a service, evaluate costs and processing durations.

Key Banking Advice:

* **Protect your valuables:** Be aware of your cash and cards since petty theft might happen.
* **Notify your bank:** To prevent notifications for suspicious behavior, let your bank know when you will be traveling.
* **Get banking applications:** With mobile banking apps, you can handle your accounts from a distance.

Beyond the Baht: Chiang Mai's Cashless Options

In Chiang Mai, cashless choices are becoming more and more popular, yet cash is still king. Mobile wallets such as PromptPay and Line Pay are gaining traction, particularly in the context of food delivery and cab services. Certain stores and eateries also accept Visa and Mastercard contactless payments.

Keep in mind:

* Before converting money, do your homework and check rates; * Be mindful of bank and ATM fees; * Always have a combination of cash and cards on hand for unexpected circumstances; Keep up with local payment options.

By using these pointers, you may confidently negotiate Chiang Mai's banking and currency scene and guarantee a hassle-free and pleasurable visit to this fascinating city. So prepare to explore the wonder of Chiang Mai by packing your luggage, exchanging your baht, and getting going!

Bonus Advice: Even though they have nothing to do with money or banking, knowing a few simple Thai words can help you communicate with locals more effectively. A little gesture of gratitude like "khob khun kha" or "mai pen rai" (no problem) may go a long way towards enhancing your experience.

SAFETY TIPS

*T*ravelers are drawn to Chiang Mai, Thailand's charming "Rose of the North," by its historic temples, lively marketplaces, and breathtaking scenery. Although typically secure, exercising prudence guarantees a worry-free and easy tour of this fascinating city. To help you explore Chiang Mai like a seasoned traveler, consider the following important safety advice:

Act Like a Street Smart:
* **Beware of pickpockets:** Congested marketplaces and popular tourist destinations like the Night Bazaar may be prime locations for small-time theft. Use a money belt, keep your valuables close at hand, and refrain from flaunting pricey devices like cameras.
* **Taxi Tip**: Use metered taxis or hail one from a hotel you can trust. Ahead of time, bargain over prices and steer clear of unauthorized cars. Red double-decker taxis, or songthaews, are less regulated but less

expensive; choose well-traveled routes or get recommendations from locals.

* **Night Wanderings:** Exercise caution if you go outside after dark. For longer trips, stick to well-lit areas, walk with company, and think about using licensed taxis.

* **Scams and Schemes:** Be cautious of abrupt "friendly encounters" that offer tours or unplanned travel aid. Refuse politely and seek advice from reliable sources of information.

Methods for Traffic:

* **Trailblazers:** The traffic in Chiang Mai may be a maze of songthaews and motorcycles. Use authorized crosswalks at all times, always check all directions before crossing, and pay more attention at night.

* **Cyclist Madness:** It may be tempting to rent a motorcycle, but be sure you are comfortable handling the busy roads and have an international driver's license. Defensive driving is essential, and helmet use is required.

* **Tango Tuk-Tuk:** These quaint motorized rickshaws are entertaining, but be sure to carefully

discuss the charge in advance to avoid paying outrageous prices. To divide the expense, think about sharing with other tourists.

Temple Precious Relics:

* **Pose the Scene:** Respect local norms by wearing modest clothes while visiting temples. Before you enter places of worship, cover your knees and shoulders and take off your shoes.

* **Keys to Etiquette:** When you're on temple property, keep your distance and behave with respect. Do not aim at statues or monks, and do not take pictures at places where signs ask not to.

Sanitization and Health:

* **Caution with Water:** In general, tap water is not safe to drink. Prior to consumption, boil tap water for at least five minutes or stick to bottled water.

* **Sun Smart:** The sun in Chiang Mai may be harsh. During peak hours, look for shade, wear hats and sunglasses, and apply sunscreen often.

* **Friends in Pharmacy:** Carry basic drugs for common conditions such as headaches and indigestion. Additionally necessary is mosquito repellant, particularly in the wet seasons.

* **Carnival of Foods:** Remain with respectable eateries that follow proper sanitation procedures. Exercise caution while consuming street food, particularly raw seafood, and choose freshly made meals over ones that have already been cooked.

A Cultural Perspective:

* **Temple Greetings:** Bow your head slightly and place your hands together at chest level to welcome monks or elders. Monks should not be touched, particularly by women.

* **Basics of Bargaining:** In marketplaces and among independent sellers, haggling is customary. Investigate reasonable costs, and when bargaining, use tact but firmness.

* *Grin and give Sawasdee a hello*: A hearty "Sawasdee" (hello) is much appreciated. It's polite to learn a few simple Thai words, such as "thank you"

(khob khun kha/khob khap), since it may improve your communication with locals.

Travel Technology:

* **Download Offline Maps:** When traveling without internet connectivity, Google Maps' offline maps come in rather handy.

* **Remain Connected:** Purchase a local SIM card to save money on calls and data. This enables you to use internet resources for suggestions and instructions as well as to keep in contact with family and friends.

* **Support It:** Make copies of your trip itinerary, prescription medications, and passport. For security, retain digital copies on a cloud-based platform.

You may confidently travel Chiang Mai and fully experience the enchantment of this alluring city by adhering to these safety precautions. Keep in mind that your greatest friends are knowledge and common sense. Thus, unwind, discover, and relish the unique splendors of Thailand's Rose of the North!

Bonus Advice: Obtain travel insurance that includes coverage for lost baggage, medical emergencies, and trip cancellations. It's an investment that delivers peace of mind and protects you against unanticipated occurrences.

Your vacation in Chiang Mai promises to be a tapestry woven with priceless memories and unique experiences if you prepare ahead of time and take a thoughtful approach. Happy travels!

CONCLUSION

As your stay in Chiang Mai comes to an end, you start to feel both nostalgic and sad. You've wandered the walls of the old city, gazed at the glistening temples, and eaten Khao Soi till your taste buds were dancing. The air is filled with the aroma of lemongrass, and your heart is filled with the sound of monks chanting. The "Rose of the North," Chiang Mai, has worked its charm, and departing is like saying goodbye to an old friend.

But remember, dear traveler, this isn't farewell, it's only "see you later." Because Chiang Mai has a way of soaking into your spirit and creating a lasting impression that calls you back. This dynamic city offers something for everyone, regardless of your interests—adventure, peace, or food.

A Time Tapestry

Take a last walk around the Old City as you say goodbye. Allow the elaborate carvings of Wat Phra Singh, a showcase for Lanna creativity, to evoke memories of former monarchs. Wat Doi Suthep's steep stairs must be ascended in order to see the expansive views that extend to Doi Inthanon National Park. Breathe in the refreshing wind that carries the murmurs of a thousand prayers given at the many shrines inside.

A Multicultural Lens

Chiang Mai is home to more than simply magnificent scenery and historic temples. It's a tapestry made of colorful cultural strands. Take in the mesmerizing moves of the Khon masked dancers as their lavish costumes, eerie music, and otherworldly surroundings carry you away. Explore the vibrant Night Bazaar, a haven for foodies and treasure seekers alike. Taste the harmonious blend of spices in Khao Soi, a rich and smooth coconut soup that envelops soft noodles and succulent chicken. Each mouthful explodes with flavor, a monument to the city's culinary brilliance.

Outside the City Barriers

Explore outside the walls of the Old City to see the lush landscape of Northern Thailand. Hike through Doi Inthanon's verdant forests to see majestic mountain peaks and tumbling waterfalls. Reestablish a connection with nature by going to an elephant sanctuary, where friendly giants wander freely. Discover the ruins of Wiang Kum Kam's fortifications and abandoned temples to get a sense of the Lanna Kingdom's majesty.

Goodbye, But Not Quite Forgotten

You may feel a wave of nostalgia wash over you as you pack your things and go to the airport. But don't be disheartened. Allow these recollections to inspire your travels and paint your fantasies. Because Chiang Mai is an experience that lasts long after you go, it's more than simply a place to visit.

*Remember this as you murmur your last "Lai Khon" (goodbye): Chiang Mai's heart beats for you. And like the vivid lotus blossom that graces its temples, it waits for your return, eager to work its enchantment once again.**

* Learn more about the rich history of the Lanna Kingdom at the Chiang Mai National Museum. * * Master Thai cookery in a traditional environment and bring your newly acquired abilities home.* **Be a valuable community contributor by volunteering at a

local NGO or elephant sanctuary.** * **Capture the spirit of Chiang Mai with pictures that are unique keepsakes of this amazing trip.

Recall that Chiang Mai is a doorway to a new way of living rather than just a place to visit. Therefore, let the Rose of the North grow in your heart long after you have left its soil by embracing the spirit of "Sabai Sabai" and taking things slow.

***Until our next encounter, Chiang Mai**.*

Made in United States
Troutdale, OR
02/22/2024

17886581R00080